CH

THE ROCKY MOUNTAINS

To Anna, our daughter,
who has explored the Rockies, among other places, with me,
and will explore many other ranges on her own

Published in 2004 by The Rosen Publishing Group, Inc.
29 East 21st Street, New York, NY 10010

First Edition

Editor: Frances E. Ruffin
Book Design: Emily Muschinske
Photo Researcher: Barbara Koppelman

Photo Credits: Cover and title page © Lester Lefkowitz/CORBIS; p. 4 © Art Wolfe/Getty Images; p. 7 © Yva Momatiuk and John Eastcott/Photo Researchers, Inc.; p. 8 (inset) © Gunter Marx/CORBIS; p. 8 © Raymond Gehman/CORBIS; p. 11 (left) © Grant V. Faint/Getty Images; p. 11 (right) © Joe McDonald/CORBIS; p. 12 (right) © Douglas Faulkner/Photo Researchers, Inc.; p. 12 (left) © Daniel Bedell/Earth Scenes; p. 15 (top) © W. Petty Conway/CORBIS; p. 15 (bottom) © Daniel J. Cox/Getty Images; p. 16 © Brian A. Vikander/CORBIS; p. 17 Denver Public Library, Western History Collection, Muriel Wolle, X61123; pp. 19, 20 © Hulton/Archive/Getty Images; p. 21 © David W. Hamilton/Getty Images.

Maynard, Charles W. (Charles William), 1955–
The Rocky Mountains / Charles W. Maynard.
    v. cm.— (Great mountain ranges of the world)
Includes bibliographical references (p.   ) and index.
Contents: Backbone of a continent—Rocks of the Rockies—Fire and ice—Snowy peaks—Life zones—Animals large and small—Scenic mountains—Exploring the Rockies—Early peoples—Protecting the Rockies today.
  ISBN 0-8239-6926-6
1. Rocky Mountains—Juvenile literature. [1. Rocky Mountains. 2. Mountains.] I. Title.
  F721 .M44 2004
  917.8—dc21
                                                                        2002013504

Manufactured in the United States of America

CONTENTS

BACKBONE OF A CONTINENT

The **rugged** Rocky Mountains are the backbone of North America. They run about 3,000 miles (4,828 km) south, from Alaska through Canada to the state of New Mexico. More than 100 smaller mountain ranges make up the Rocky Mountain chain.

The Rockies form part of North America's Continental Divide, which is a line of the highest points in North America. The Continental Divide separates many rivers that flow east from those that flow west. These rivers begin on the high peaks of the Rockies. They include the Rio Grande and the Mackenzie, Saskatchewan, Missouri, Snake, Columbia, Colorado, and Arkansas Rivers.

The Rocky Mountain chain takes its name from its many treeless, rocky peaks. Mount Elbert in Colorado is the highest peak in the Rockies at 14,433 feet (4,399 m). The chain can be divided into five sections, the Southern, Middle, Northern, Canadian, and Brooks Ranges. In Canada, the Rockies rise up as a solid wall that once made it difficult for European settlers to travel through them.

Glacier National Park, Montana, which is in the Rocky Mountain chain, is home to many plants and animals, such as this mountain goat. Glacier National Park is located along the Continental Divide.

THE ANCIENT ROCKIES

Parts of the Rocky Mountains were built in different ways. Some were volcanic rocks formed under an ancient sea more than one billion years ago. They were caught between large, moving plates of Earth's **crust**. These rocks were pushed up into high mountains. They were later flattened by **erosion**. This allowed ancient seas to roll across the land and to leave **sediments** of sand and clay, which hardened into rock. More than 75 million years ago, pressure from below Earth's crust pushed these rocks up into great rugged mountain ranges. About 40 million years ago, what we know as the Rocky Mountains were again raised thousands of feet (m). Then, 600,000 years ago, the heat and pressure of mountain building caused volcanoes to erupt, mostly in the Montana and Wyoming area. Over time, rivers and streams have carved out canyons and steep, narrow valleys.

MOUNTAIN FACT

THE ROCKY MOUNTAIN TRENCH IS A SERIES OF NARROW VALLEYS ON THE WESTERN SIDE OF THE ROCKIES IN CANADA AND NORTHWESTERN UNITED STATES. THE TRENCH RUNS ABOUT 900 MILES (1,448 KM) FROM THE YUKON RIVER IN BRITISH COLUMBIA TO FLATHEAD LAKE IN WESTERN MONTANA.

The Bighorn River flows through Devil's Canyon in Wyoming and Montana's Bighorn National Recreation Area.

Fire and Ice

Volcanoes have erupted in the Rockies for millions of years. The area also has many hot spots where **magma** from far below Earth's crust rises to near the surface. Hot springs, bubbling mud pots, **geysers**, and fumaroles, or cracks in the Earth from which steam erupts, are signs of the hot activity below the ground. Many hot spots are found in Yellowstone National Park, in Montana, Wyoming, and Idaho, and in Banff National Park in Alberta, Canada. One geyser, Old Faithful in Yellowstone, is famous for its regular eruptions of steam. Since the 1800s, hot springs in Banff have attracted visitors who bathe in the warm waters.

In addition to volcanoes, **glaciers** have shaped the mountains into the Rockies that we see today. Glaciers are slow-moving rivers of ice that carve *U*-shaped valleys. The northern U.S. and Canadian Rockies have many glaciers that continue to wear down the high mountains. As the glaciers melt, they form beautiful lakes and rushing rivers, as well as rocky ridges or hills called moraines.

 Old Faithful, a geyser in Yellowstone National Park, erupts steam from 90 to 184 feet (27–56 m) into the air about every 85 minutes. Inset: Bathers enjoy the hot springs in the Canadian Rockies at the Banff National Park in Alberta.

A Range of Climates

The climate in the Rocky Mountain range changes greatly. The highest peaks stay covered in snow year-round. One snow-covered range in Colorado has been called the Never Summer Mountains because its peaks remain snow-capped throughout the year. Peaks that are 1,000 miles (1,609 km) south and are at lower **elevations** near the hot desert of New Mexico lose their snow during the summer.

The Rockies receive very little **precipitation**. Most of the moisture comes as snow in the winter. This snow melts in the spring, and by the summer it provides much-needed water for the valleys and plains. The western ranges of the Rockies have more precipitation than have those in the east. Weather clouds from the Pacific Ocean move inland and hit the western side of the Rockies. Moisture from these clouds cools and drops rain or snow.

MOUNTAIN

Avalanches are masses of ice and snow that suddenly move down the steep sides of a mountain. Some of these snow slides may sweep down a mountainside at speeds close to 200 miles per hour (322 km/h)

Top: *Ship-Rock Peak rises from a desert in New Mexico.* Bottom: *Hayden Valley in Yellowstone National Park is covered with snow.*

PLANT LIFE ZONES

Forest fires are common in the dry Rockies region. After a fire, large stands of lodgepole pines will grow in a burned-out area. Forest fires help lodgepole pines to **reproduce**. Heat from the fire opens the pinecones so that they can spread their seeds. Eighty-five percent of the trees in Yellowstone National Park are lodgepole pines.

There are three zones of plant life in the Rockies. In the **montane** zone, 5,600 to 9,500 feet (1,707 –2,896 m) above **sea level**, lodgepole and ponderosa pines grow. In the **subalpine zone** at about 9,500 to 11,000 feet (2,896–3,353), Engelmann spruce and subalpine fir trees grow. The **alpine zone**, 11,000 feet (3,353 m) and above, has a very cold climate where no trees grow. The plants that grow there are very low to the ground to stay out of the cold winds. Mosses, grasses, and wildflowers are common. Some wildflowers have hairs on their stems and leaves to protect them from the cold winds. These flowers are often red and purple to take in and hold the heat of the sun better.

 Left: *Wildflowers grow high on Alpine Peak near Ouray, Colorado.* Inset: *These young lodgepole pines have grown after a forest fire in Yellowstone National Park.*

Rocky Mountain Animals

Compared to other parts of North America, the Rockies have few people living in them. For this reason, many animals such as moose, elk, bighorn sheep, grizzly bears, Rocky Mountain goats, black bears, and bison take **refuge** there. Coyotes, mountain lions, and wolves search for food, along the forested slopes. Smaller animals such as yellow-bellied marmots, pikas, tufted-ear Aberts squirrels, otters, and beavers are at home on the rocky slopes and in the streams of the mountains.

Some animals such as the Rocky Mountain goat live in the highest mountains. These surefooted "goats" are actually antelopes that like the steep cliffs of the Rockies. Many birds also live in these mountains. The golden eagle can be seen soaring above peaks throughout the chain. The bald eagle, the national bird of the United States, also lives on cliffs high above the rivers and lakes of the Rockies.

MOUNTAIN FACT

GRIZZLY BEARS LIVE IN THE ROCKIES FROM ALASKA TO NEVADA. GRIZZLIES ARE SOME OF THE LARGEST BEARS IN THE WORLD. THESE HUGE ANIMALS CAN WEIGH FROM 224 TO 714 POUNDS (102–324 KG). THEY CAN EAT UP TO 90 POUNDS (41 KG) OF BERRIES, FISH, AND OTHER FOODS PER DAY.

 The American bald eagle is found only in North America. These eagles can ride on columns of air called thermals. They fly at average speeds of 30 miles per hour (48 km/h).

 A grizzly bear does not hibernate, or sleep through the winter, but it may take long naps in a cave or a dead tree. However, beware, it is easily awakened.

Ranch hands, also known as cowboys, ride among a herd of grazing cattle during a cattle drive in the Big Belt Mountains of Montana.

A Rich Economy

The Rockies pass through two Canadian **provinces** and nine U.S. states. In Canada, the Rockies are part of British Columbia and Alberta. In the United States, peaks rise in New Mexico, Arizona, Colorado, Utah, Nevada, Wyoming, Idaho, Montana, and Alaska.

During the 1850s and 1860s, European settlers first passed through the Rockies on their way to California and Oregon in search of gold and good farmland. By the late 1800s, the mountains were found to be rich in gold, silver, and copper. Today, mining for coal and minerals, as well as drilling for oil and gas, are major **industries**. Cattle and sheep ranching are also important parts of the economy in the mountain region. Every year, millions of people visit the Rockies and the national parks located there. People go to the Rockies to ski, to hike, to mountain climb, and to enjoy the region's natural beauty.

This photograph of a Colorado silver mine owner was taken between 1900 and 1910.

EXPLORING THE ROCKIES

In 1804 and 1806, Meriwether Lewis and William Clark led an **expedition** through the Rockies to find a water route to the Pacific Ocean. Although they did not find a route based entirely on rivers, they did explore the mountains and meet many Native Americans who lived there. Zebulon Pike explored the southern Rockies from 1805 to 1807. Pikes Peak in Colorado stands at 14,110 feet (4,301 m) and is named for this early explorer.

Other explorers hunted for beaver skins for the hats worn by men at that time. Fur trappers, also called mountain men, mapped mountain routes and led expeditions through the Rockies. These men included Jedediah Smith, Jim Bridger, and Kit Carson. Their efforts helped thousands of people to travel west through the South Pass. At 7,550 feet (2,301 m) high, this pass in the Oregon Trail was a grassy route through the Rocky Mountains.

MOUNTAIN FACT

IN 1871, FERDINAND HAYDEN LED AN EXPEDITION TO THE YELLOWSTONE REGION OF THE ROCKIES. IN 1872, LARGELY THROUGH HAYDEN'S EFFORTS, YELLOWSTONE BECAME THE WORLD'S FIRST NATIONAL PARK.

In May 1869, in Promontory, Utah, the last spike was driven into the track of the transcontinental railroad, the first railroad to cross the nation.

This photograph of a Blackfoot chief and his family traveling by horseback was taken in 1890.

EARLY PEOPLES

Humans have lived in and around the Rockies for thousands of years. Some Native American groups that hunted in the mountains were the Blackfoot, the Shoshone, the Ute, the Arapaho, the Pueblo, and the Apache. **Descendants** of those early peoples still live in the Rockies. Many live on lands called **reservations**, or communities specially set aside by the government for native people.

As settlers moved into the Rockies, disagreements over rights to land and other matters broke out between the Native Americans and the settlers. Native Americans hunted in the Rockies for food to **survive**, and the settlers hunted for furs, dug mines, and cut timber. This conflict was a dark time in the history of North America, when many people, mainly Native Americans, were killed and were forced to leave their land.

A modern-day Ute Indian chief and his son dance at Ute Mountain Tribal Park in Colorado.

Protecting the Rockies Today

Every year millions of people travel roads, tunnels, and railroads to reach the great Rocky Mountains. Many of them visit U.S. and Canadian national parks. These parks were established by governments in both countries to preserve and protect the wildlife and scenery for everyone to enjoy.

Scientists are working with park rangers to protect animals such as bison, bighorn sheep, grizzly bears, and gray wolves. Gray wolves once roamed the central Rockies of Wyoming. From the late 1800s through the early 1900s, humans hunted gray wolves until they had disappeared from the area. To help the wolves to become familiar with the region again, scientists captured pairs of these animals in the Canadian Rockies and moved them to Idaho and to Yellowstone National Park. The wolves are doing well in their new homes.

Fires, such as the ones that burned in Yellowstone in 1988, burn large areas of the mountain forests. Scientists continue to study the effect fires have on forest **ecology**. Many think that natural fires started by lightning can help forests to stay healthy. The Rockies are being studied all the time to understand Earth and people's effect on the **environment**.

GLOSSARY

alpine zone (AL-pyn ZOHN) The life zone above the treeline.

crust (KRUST) The outer, or top, layer of a planet.

descendants (dih-SEN-dentz) People born of a certain family or group.

ecology (ee-KAH-luh-jee) The study of how living things are linked with each other and with Earth.

elevations (eh-luh-VAY-shunz) Height of objects.

environment (en-VY-ern-ment) All the living things and conditions of a place.

erosion (ih-ROH-zhun) The wearing away of land over time.

expedition (ek-spuh-DIH-shun) A trip for a special purpose.

geysers (GY-zerz) Eruptions of hot water and steam from cracks in Earth's surface.

glaciers (GLAY-shurz) Large masses of ice that move down a mountain or along a valley.

industries (IN-dus-treez) A moneymaking business in which many people work and make money
    producing a particular product.

magma (MAG-muh) A hot, liquid rock beneath Earth's surface.

montane (mon-TAYN) Having to do with mountains.

precipitation (preh-sih-pih-TAY-shun) Any moisture that falls from the sky.

provinces (PRAH-vins-ez) The main parts of a country.

refuge (REH-fyooj) A place that gives shelter or protection.

reproduce (ree-pruh-DOOS) To make more of something.

reservations (reh-zer-VAY-shunz) Lands set aside by the government for Native Americans to
    live on.

rugged (RUH-gid) Covered with rough edges.

sea level (SEE LEH-vul) The height of the top of the ocean.

sediments (SEH-dih-ments) Gravel, sand, silt, or mud carried by wind or water.

subalpine zone (sub-AL-pyn ZOHN) The life zone just below the alpine zone.

survive (sur-VYV) To live longer than; to stay alive.

Index

Web Sites

Due to the changing nature of Internet links, PowerKids Press has developed an online list of Web sites related to the subject of this book. This site is updated regularly. Please use this link to access the list:

www.powerkidslinks.com/gmrw/rockymo/